How To
Get Yourself
An "Honest-To-GOD"
Grant!

Yes! They Really **DO** Exist!

Dennis Lively
Author of The Best Sellers...
"Unleash Your Business" and "How To Survive The Upcoming Funding Crunch"

Table Of Contents

Foreword

Let's get this book started out on the right foot...with the truth! We've all seen those late-night TV commercials with the guy in the funny jacket telling us that all of our money problems can be solved by simply getting a government grant.

"Get a grant to start a business, write a book, buy a house...scratch your nose! A government grant will solve all of your problems. Just send $69.95 to the address at the bottom of your screen and start raking in the money!"

Does that sound a little too good to be true? I know; I wish it were all true, too! The fact of the matter is, there IS some truth hiding in there.

The Federal Government DOES grant over $30 BILLION dollars every year. Unfortunately, the VAST majority of those funds go to "County governments, City or township governments, Independent school districts, State controlled institutions of higher education, Native American tribal governments (Federally recognized), Nonprofits other than institutions of higher education [includes community action agencies and other organizations having a 501(c)(3) status with the IRS], Private institutions of higher education, State governments ". By the vast majority, I mean over 95% of that money goes to the organizations listed above. Is your family one of those organizations?

Private foundations and trusts also grant over 20 BILLION dollars every year. Again, the vast majority goes to non-profit organizations, schools, libraries and universities. So, that leaves you out of the game again.

Don't let all of this discourage you! I promised you the truth and that is the truth. You don't qualify for the vast majority of Federal and Private grants!

Did you notice that I said, "Federal"? There are grants available at the state level that you can apply for and actually receive. This is where I hope to focus your efforts throughout this book.

Did you also notice that I said, "the VAST majority"? There are a few...very few...Federal and Private grants that you may be eligible for. I will point these grants out to you as we go along. You need to know that this type of grant is very limited in focus and is always very competitive. They are attainable though.

So...if you thought you would buy this book, fill out a few forms and get a big check from Uncle Sam, you need to think about that a bit. If it was that easy, don't you think everyone would be receiving grant money? Do you know anyone who has received a grant?

Well, you might well be the first one on your block! You CAN receive grant funds. You just have to know where to look and what to do and who to talk to. You have to use a "laser beam" focus instead of a shotgun approach. This book will point you in the right direction, give you the right information and tools and walk you step-by step through the process. It truly can "Unleash Your Life."

So, what do you say? You've heard the truth, are you ready to get started? GOOD! Let's go!

Chapter One: Grants, Entitlements and Loans

Let's get some terms straight so we are all on the same page. It may well be that you need an entitlement rather than a grant, or that there are no grants available but there are loans that will fill your needs. If you don't know the difference, then you'll never get the money you are looking for.

Grants are just that; you get money that you never have to pay back. As we talked about in the foreword, most grants just aren't for the "average joe". However, there are still grants that you can receive. Every grant always comes with conditions. For example, " If you meet the following qualifications, AND prove a need, AND present a compelling proposal, AND present an accurate budget, AND allow us to check on your progress, AND send us proof of the outcome, THEN we will put you in competition for this grant.

See what I mean by conditions. That sounds like a lot of stuff to get through. It is, in a way, but we'll walk through that together when we get into the process of getting a grant.

Just for now, you need to know that a grant is money that you will never pay back to anyone. It is money that is given to you after you agree to some conditions. It is money that is given after competing grant applications are compared to each other. The winning grant applications get the money.

You may think of entitlements as benefits. Some common examples of entitlements are:

Social Security

Medicare

Unemployment

Worker's Compensation

Entitlements are simply programs that, if you qualify, will pay you money or provide services for you.

The key to entitlements is that there are a TON of them! You may qualify for several and not even know it.

Did you know you might be entitled to free winterization of your home? Or free mechanical upgrades for your car? Or even free help with your utilities? Entitlements are there for everyone in the United States. You just have to know where to look for them and what it takes to qualify for them.

We'll spend a whole chapter on entitlements later on in this book, but for now just know that entitlements are benefits that you may be qualified to receive AND That there are a LOT of them.

Loans are an entirely different book. Loans are money that you have to pay back. There is an interest charge, even though it is usually lower than you can get elsewhere. There are federally guaranteed loans for just about any purpose. If you are starting a business, there is a low, cost, minimum requirement loan for you. If you are going to college, there are loans for you. If you are buying a house, there's a loan.

You get the idea. Loans are a way to get money fairly easily, with not a lot of hassles. They do take some paperwork and some preparation, but they are available virtually for everyone.

So, you have three basic ways to get money for your family. Grants, Entitlements and Loans. Now comes the question, which is right for you?

We'll start on that in the next chapter.

Chapter Two: Which One is Right For Me?

Well, that depends on your individual situation. Let's talk it out and see which way of getting some extra money for your family's goals is most appropriate for you.

1. If you need the money right away and your family has an income above the Federal Poverty Line, (see below) a loan is probably the right way for you to go. You probably don't qualify for very many, if any, entitlements and a grant is a longer process than you want to undertake if you need the money quickly. Check the following chart to see where your family stands.

2011 HHS Poverty Guidelines Persons in Family

48 Contiguous States and D.C.	Alaska	Hawaii
1 $10,890	$13,600	$12,540
2 14,710	18,380	16,930
3 18,530	23,160	21,320
4 22,350	27,940	25,710
5 26,170	32,720	30,100
6 29,990	37,500	34,490
7 33,810	42,280	38,880
8 37,630	47,060	43,270
For each additional person, add		
3,820	4,780	4,390

Most entitlement programs use 150% of the Federal Poverty Guidelines to qualify you. So, if you have a family of 3 and make below $23,160.00 a year, you may qualify for some entitlements. If you fit this category, take a look at Chapter 3 and see if there are entitlement programs that will help you.

If your family income puts you well above the guidelines, you may want to look at guaranteed federal loan programs. These programs are a little more restrictive about what you can use the money for, but the process is fairly simple and fairly quick. If you fit into this category, see Chapter 4 for more details.

The ideal situation for receiving a grant is when you don't really need the money immediately. Grants take a while! If you are making it day to day and have some time to wait, then a grant is for you.

Most grants are awarded twice a year, some are awarded quarterly. Almost all of them have a grant deadline. If you miss it, you will wait to apply at the beginning of the next grant cycle. This could mean waiting as much as a year to reapply.

There are a few grants, most of them at the state level, that are awarded constantly. These tend to be grants for very specific things, like the arts, music, educational activities, that sort of thing. If you qualify for this type of grant, the process is very short.

So, it all boils down to how quickly you need the money AND how much money you have now. If you are having an emergency, laid-off, injured, unemployed, then look at entitlements first. You can get help almost immediately, if qualified.

If you are looking long term and have the day-to-day expenses covered, then look to a grant or loan.

The next chapter will tell you about entitlements and where to find which ones may apply to your situation. You will find resources to research the entitlement programs, both on a Federal and state level. You will also find out how to tell if you qualify for these entitlements.

Chapter 4 will talk about loans that may be just right for your situation.

Chapter 5 will start our process of getting a grant.

These first few chapters are very important. You need to know which type of funding to pursue or you will be wasting a LOT of time and effort and not getting any money for your trouble.

So, let's take a quick look at entitlements to see if they fit your situation.

Chapter Three: Entitlements

First of all, take a look at the Federal Poverty Guidelines I placed back in Chapter Two. Figure 150% of those incomes. If your family income is less than or even $1000 above those guidelines, you may be qualified for a lot of entitlements. If your income is greatly higher than the guidelines, just skim this chapter and go on. I ask you to read it because you may run into someone that entitlements CAN help and YOU would be able to supply some information to them. It really gives you a good feeling...try it!

If it looks like you may fall in, or close to, the guidelines, then go to: http://www.firstgov.gov/Citizen/Topics/Benefits.shtml

There, you will find an exhaustive list of entitlements/benefits . Click around and research any that may apply to your situation. The qualifications are right there. You can see for yourself if you are eligible or not. You can also read about the program and see if it will give you the help you are looking for.

You can also go to: http://www.govbenefits.gov/index.jsp

On that page, you are given two choices to search. The one on the left let's you answer questions and then the program will find benefits that fit your answers. The one on the right just lets you search without answering any questions. It's your choice. Both will give you great results.

Another, and perhaps the best, resource for entitlements/benefits is your local Department of Health and Human Resources. Nearly every county in the nation has one. Call them and make an appointment. They are there to help you and do an excellent job at it.

Entitlements aren't for everyone or for every purpose. Do some research and see if they fit your needs. If they do, jump in and get started. The programs work! If they don't fit your needs, read on...there's more information coming!

Chapter Four: Loans

There are all types of loans. The ones that we will discuss here are federally or state guaranteed. You may also just go to a bank or re-mortgage your home. The rates are very low right now and this may seem appealing. Just remember, you are putting your house up for collateral.

If you are looking for a loan to start a business or expand an existing business, I humbly refer you to my book, "Unleash Your Business". It is written in the same style as this book. It walks you through the process step-by-step. Of course, I highly recommend it!

If you need money for college, try your local school guidance counselor. They have piles of information.

Loans are not typically a long-term fix of a problem. They are more of a tool to get out of a problem and get started over, or just get started period. So be careful with loans for a family problem. They may just end up hurting you more in the long run.

However, if you are starting a business, a loan is THE vehicle for you.

Just a short chapter on the pros and cons so that you can make a choice of which way you want to go in your search to "Unleash Your Life".

Let's make that choice in the next chapter.

Chapter Five: The Choice Is Up To You

Well, by now you have enough information to be able to make an intelligent choice about which way to proceed in your quest to get some extra money for your family. I hope you've done some thinking about it. Looked at the pros and cons of each way to get some extra money and compared them to your own personal situation.

To recap: if you need immediate help and you don't make a whole lot of money, go the entitlement route. The people at the Department of Health and Human resources will be glad to help you. The process is short and you get the help you need almost immediately.

If you are looking to start a business or go to college, go for a loan. The college loans don't usually require a total refinancing of your home and the business loans may accept things like computer equipment, furniture, etc. as collateral. The process is a bit longer, but very easily managed with some help.

If you really don't NEED the money but want to think long-term for your family, then the grant process fits you well. Just know that this is not a quick process and takes some preparation.

The remainder of this book is devoted to the grant process. Even if you have decided to go with one of the other two processes, keep this book. It has great information that will help you in a number of ways.

Chapter Six: This Grant's For You

Okay! So, you've looked at your funding options and decided that a grant is the one that fits your needs the best. Let's get started on getting you that grant money.

You've made the first step in your journey. The next step is to narrow down things a little bit.

You want a grant. What for? What services are you going to render to others that will justify the government giving you money? What can you do that merits getting free money? Tough question, right?

Here's a list of things that are generally covered by grants:

1. Research into new technologies
2. Development of new technologies
3. Transferring new technologies to the marketplace

These first 3 activities are paid for from the federal budget. We'll have a chapter on just these activities in a little while.

4. Sing for the public
5. Play music for the public
6. Dance for the public
7. Act for the public
8. Tell jokes for the public

9. Read poetry for the public

10. Read about historical figures for the public

11. Do a craft for the public

12. Teach a seminar for the public

13. Help a public group get organized

14. Help a public group market itself

The list can go on and on. You get the idea. You do something for the public that will teach them something, make their lives better or entertain them and the government will pay you to do it.

I personally know a lady who makes over $20,000.00 a year impersonating Mary Todd Lincoln. She studied up on the former first lady, got some authentic looking dresses, put together a one hour monologue speaking in "her voice" and now travels throughout a 3 state area being Mary Todd Lincoln on weekends only. The state governments give her $20,000.00 a year plus expenses to do this. Not bad for a second job...she's a cook at a high school!

I give you this example to open your mind a bit. You don't have to be a world-class performer or artist or scientist to get a grant. You just have to do your research and see what actions the state you live in is giving grants for. Can you teach someone to work on automobiles? Can you be an historical figure for an hour? Can you show a group how to set up their accounting system?

The secret is to look at what is getting funded now and tailor your grant application accordingly. This important first step will save you a LOT of time and effort and frustration. Why re-invent the wheel when it is already rolling down the road?

I'm NOT saying copy ideas! Just use those ideas as a springboard to your own approach to providing services to the residents of your state and perhaps neighboring states. That's the NUMBER ONE secret to getting a grant!

How do you start this process? You do some research on your state. Nearly all grants are funded at the state level. It just makes sense to start there.

Here is a great website to start your research. Just click to find your state and then go to the "Arts" section. Go ahead and look at the other sections for your state, too. You are specifically looking for any mention of grants.

http://www.statelocalgov.net/index.cfm

I just did a search for Alabama, the first one I came to, and came up with a TON of grants for $5000.00! Now you need to do the same thing for your state and bordering states. See what they are interested in funding and write down any that look interesting to you. Remember, you don't have to be a master artist or musician or actor.

Play around in the site I gave you above. Look at the possibilities and MAKE A LIST.

We'll get back together and start the next step when you get that finished. See you in a while.

Chapter Seven: I've Got A Few Ideas

I thought that website I gave you in the last chapter would get your brain working! I hope you've come up with 3 or 4 ideas for a grant. Now we need to pick out just one to work with.

"Why don't I just apply for all 5 of them?" you ask.

Well, if you notice, a lot of the grants are administered by the same department of state government. If you send 5 different grant applications to the same department, you'll really confuse them! It's a lot better strategy to get one grant approved, or in the process of being approved, before you ask for more money. It's even a better idea to fully complete one grant, ask to extend that one and send in a new project at that time. The state department you're working with will have a track record with you and are much more likely to re-fund your first grant AND fund your new grant at the same time.

Does that make sense? Think long term.

Now, you've got a few ideas that are interesting to you. You need to pick JUST ONE! Make it the one you are most comfortable with, the one you like the best. You are going to be living with this grant for a while, so you'd better like it!

Pick one and let's move on!

Chapter Eight: First Steps

Okay, you've got your project idea, now let's get a grant application started. There are a few things that are common to every grant application. The grant you apply for from your state will probably have a few more requirements. We'll get to some of those in a minute. First, let's go over the basics.

Before you even start on the paperwork, you have to do some work yourself. I'll use Mary Todd Lincoln as an example. Before the lady even applied for the grant, she studied up on Mary Todd Lincoln and wrote an outline of what her presentation would cover. She then started practicing her presentation and taped it each time. She went out and found the costume she would be wearing during the presentation. She then videotaped herself actually doing the complete presentation in costume. She had this ready BEFORE she even touched an application form.

I am just using Mary Todd Lincoln as an example. Whatever you have decided to pursue as a grant project, do the work upfront. Have a finished product before you apply. You'll see that every grant requires, at the very least, a detailed explanation of your proposed project. Many want a sample of it, so Mary Todd Lincoln's video was definitely a winner. This process will also let you see if the project fits you...if this is something you would enjoy doing.

Don't make the mistake of just filling out the application and trying to BS your way through the Project Summary. It will be obvious to the people who review the applications. Do the work upfront!

After you have your project designed and ready, go get the application form from the department you are going to be working with in your state. Most states have the forms online so that you can just download it and print it out. Download it now and print yourself about 5 copies. Read over it and understand it.

Some of the forms will ask for your project summary on the form itself. It is usually very important to keep these summaries brief and to the point. If the form asks you for more detail or gives you an option for additional sheets, write out a detailed project summary similar to the example I've placed on the next page.

For that example, I've used another friend of mine. He travels around the state, again on the weekends, and helps craft businesses organize their businesses and setup a simple bookkeeping system. Last year, he made an extra $12,000.00 by doing that. Plus, he got to meet some great people, stay in some areas of the state that he had never been in and had his expenses paid. Not a bad deal!

Use the example as just that, an example! You have to personalize it to your project, of course. Put it in your own words so that your enthusiasm for the project comes through.

Here's the example.

Chapter Nine: An Example Project Summary

The Craft of Business For Crafters
Project Summary

After some personal research, I have come to the conclusion that the vast majority of crafters in our state are very talented and passionate artists. However, they are usually not so talented when it comes to business practices.

I propose to remedy that situation by offering my considerable business knowledge to crafters throughout the state. I will accomplish this by holding free seminars for crafters where we would go into detail about all of the following topics:

A simple bookkeeping system

Are you making money on that item?

Best business practices

Business rules and regulations

How to market effectively

Do I need to be on the Internet?

There are 14 more topics included in the course outline I have included with this application.

I am certain that, with some simple fine-tuning, our crafter community in this state would be more vibrant, more profitable and perhaps be able to create more job opportunities as they grow.

I propose to offer this service free of charge to all crafters in our state.

In my proposed budget, I have figured 1 seminar a weekend for 52 weeks. The amount I am requesting reflects my minimal travel expenses and 4 actual hours of instructional time plus the cost of paper handouts given to the seminar attendees.

My project also entails follow-up with these crafters by phone, mail and email to reinforce the lessons and to track the program's effectiveness.

A project end report will record all of this data in order to monitor and record our success as well as tweak the program to make it more effective in following years.

After a reasonable amount of grant- supported seminars, the program would have a track record of successes and could start to charge a small fee from each crafter attending the seminars. This would lead to the program being self-sufficient in future years.

In summary, "The Craft of Business For Crafters" would have a positive affect on our crafter community by allowing them to be more organized, more legally compliant and, most importantly, more profitable.

I have included a course outline as well as a videotape of me actually holding a seminar for crafters in my county.

I urge you to approve this grant. It will make a huge difference to the crafters of our state.

See what I did with the summary? I didn't try to explain the whole project. I hit the highlights. I said enough to get them to read the rest of the application.

That's an important point. Let the application work as a whole; don't try to make the different parts of it sell the whole thing.

The Project Summary is just that, a summary. Use it to spark interest. Interest enough to read the whole application. The people who screen these applications see them all day. You need to make them want to read yours and hopefully put it on top of the pile!

You should also notice that I referenced the additional items I included with the application...the course outline and a videotape. This gets across the fact that these are an important part of the application and should be taken into account.

The Project Summary is your foot in the door. Make sure that you make a good first impression. Use your Spell-Checker. Make it sound professional. Be enthusiastic and positive. Use words like "will" instead of "would", they sort of take for granted that the grant "will" be approved and the program "will" work. A very subtle thing, but very effective. If you are thinking, "would" it means "maybe"... doesn't sound too positive, does it?

So, your first project is to write your Project Summary. Get enthusiastic, get positive and get it done!

Chapter Ten: Your Project Budget

The most important piece of paper contained in your grant application, at least to the people making the grant, is your Project Budget.

Every department that awards grants has a budget they have to work within. They have to work hard to get the money from the state legislature. They have to be able to show the politicians results! So, the departments are very dollar conscious.

Some departments have certain levels of funding. The most I have ever seen awarded to an individual is $20,000.00. Most departments have, for example, a $5000.00 and $10,000.00 program and not anything in between. So, if your Project Budget comes in at $7,500.00 it doesn't fit.

Do some research and see what levels the department you are planning to apply to offers. This will help you set up your budget accordingly. It's simply not real smart to ask for more money than they are prepared to grant.

It's also a good idea to look around their site and see if they have a list of grants awarded in previous years. This is very instructive in that you can see what has been successful in the past and how much money was awarded.

Again, try to work within their comfort zone as much as possible. The department budgets are very tight right now, so they are not very apt to take a whole lot of chances with the money they do have.

Okay, after you've done a little research on funding levels, it's time to start on your project budget. You need to be able to justify every dollar you ask for...and justify it on the state's terms.

A simple example that nearly everyone messes up is this. The Federal Guidelines for travel expense is somewhere around 50 cents a mile. (It actually went up to 51 cents in 2011). Most states do not use that figure! I've seen everything from 40 cents to 55 cents. You need to see what your state figures mileage reimbursement at. You can usually find this through a Google search. To be safe, if you can't find it, use 50 cents a mile.

I've included a sample project budget in the next chapter.

Just remember, when you are doing your budget, don't go crazy! Be conservative with your figures. You can bet that the people who are reviewing your application will be very conservative!

You need to list things like mileage, your time, printed materials you will need, special equipment, (like slide projectors, sound equipment, etc). Anything you would use exclusively for your project.

A great tip about this: If you need a sound system (or anything) for your project and you already have one, put the amount you paid for the piece of equipment into your budget with an asterisk after it. Then write that you have already purchased this item. It shows your commitment to the project! Always helps the approval process. Here's the Example Project Budget. On the next page.

Chapter Eleven: A Sample Project Budget

Project: The Craft Of Business For Crafters

Start Date: July 1, 2003

End Date June 30, 2004

Assumptions:

    1 seminar weekly for 52 weeks

    1 paid local newspaper ad for each seminar

    Maximum mileage charged: 200 miles one way

Budget:

Newspaper ads:	52 ads X $8.00	$ 416.00
Mileage:	400 miles X 52 X .30	$ 6240.00
Slide Projector: **		$ 300.00
Handouts: 1000 X .05		$ 50.00
Instructional Time 208 hours X 15.00		$ 3120.00
Misc. Costs		$ 174.00

Total Budget: $10,000.00

    ** I have already purchased this item in anticipation of using it in this project. It is not added into the budget.

The budget is pretty straightforward. You will notice I put a cap on how much mileage I would charge. If you live in a big state like Texas or California, you will probably want to adjust this accordingly.

I also discounted my time drastically. In the majority of state grants, you make most of your money in mileage reimbursements. In the example budget, it was over 60% of the budget.

In this example, the state had a limit of $10,000.00. If I had valued my time at my usual rate of $50 an hour, the hourly rate alone would have busted the budget!

I have found over the years that state departments understand mileage well... they deal with it on a daily basis. Most of them get reimbursed for their mileage when they travel on state business. They are in their comfort zone!

When you start talking about $50 an hour...that's a whole different ballgame! The majority of state workers make under $15 an hour and can understand that figure. $50 an hour seems outrageous to them. Again, their comfort zone.

Did you notice the asterisk? It works!

Now go on and start on your budget. Remember to stay within the funding levels established by your state. AND to stay within their comfort zones!

See you back here in a little bit.

Chapter Twelve: Tracking The Outcome

If you just gave someone $10,000.00, wouldn't you want to see what you got for your money? Your state does, also. They just LOVE tracking outcomes. As a matter of fact, most of them require you to track how well your project did. That makes sense.

BUT, you have to show a tracking mechanism as part of your grant application. A few states don't expressly require this, but you can bet your last dollar they are impressed when they get a method to track their investment.

Again, budgets are tight in almost every state. The departments have to justify their grants to the legislature. Tracking methods from you help them in that task. You help them; they are more apt to help you!

Tracking can be as simple or as complicated as you want to make it. An example of a simple system would be keeping a list of people who attended your "Mary Todd Lincoln" presentation and getting some comments from a few of them.

That's exactly the tracking done for the real world "Mary Todd Lincoln" project. That worked well!

The "Craft of Business" project used a little more sophisticated tracking. That guy tracked profits after the seminar in comparison with profits before the seminar. This, too, was very successful.

An example tracking strategy follows.

Chapter Thirteen: An Example Tracking Strategy

In order to show that the "Mary Todd Lincoln" Project is effective in its task of bringing history alive to the people of this state, I have developed the following method to track its effectiveness.

1. I will keep a complete list of names and addresses of each person who attends a presentation.

2. These lists will be broken down into Senatorial Districts to allow our legislators a view of the good things that this project is bringing to their district.

3. I will also hand out and get back comment forms from the audiences. These forms will also be handled as above.

4. I will keep receipts of every expenditure covered by this grant and turn then into the department for accountability of every grant dollar.

5. I will make myself available, at anytime, for interim checks of the project status.

6. I will faithfully, and in a timely manner, complete and return all forms required by the state to complete this grant.

Now, that's not really too hard! Just show how you plan to prove to them that they are getting their money's worth from your project.

I hope you notice that I tied in the politicians. This is very important! The money comes to the departments from them. If you send the department a list of attendees, who do you think they will send that list to??

Yep! The legislators. With a note saying, "Look what we did for the voters in YOUR district!"

The legislators, if they are smart, will turn around and send out a letter asking their constituents how they liked the Mary Todd Lincoln show that they made possible. See how it works?

I also put in a section that deals with the forms the state wants from you at the end of the grant. This is a huge problem for a lot of states! People just don't turn these grant closing forms in. Don't even start that! You can almost be assured of never getting another grant if you do! By stating that in your tracking, you are saying that you recognize this problem and won't be a part of it. Again, comfort zone!

That's really all there is to tracking. Make it show numbers that will be important to the department AND the politicians

It's time to put the application together and move on to the really important parts.

Chapter Fourteen: Putting the Application Together

Okay! We've got everything we need to get the application in the mail. Pat yourself on the back. Good job so far. Not a lot of people make it this far.

You've figured out that you need a grant, not a loan or an entitlement. You've done your research on your state's grant situation, who's giving grants and what for. You've narrowed down the grant possibilities to one that really appeals to you.

You've written a project summary, a project budget and a project tracking strategy.

Now, let's put it all together.

Get the grant application and fill it out completely. DON'T LEAVE ANY BLANKS! When you leave a blank, some staff member at the department you are applying to has to figure out what goes in there, or even worse, puts your application back in the mail to tell you to fill in the missing information. I've missed grants this way...I know!

If they asked for the grant to be typed, type it! Again, let's stay in that comfort zone we talked about.

You should have an application form, a project summary, a project budget, a project tracking strategy and any supporting material you have decided to add...the course outline or video, for example.

Some states will have other forms you need to fill out when applying. They are always either on the Internet site or in the package you get in the mail from the department. Make sure you fill out and return every required form. Don't get put in that big "incomplete" file.

Make sure your package has PLENTY of time to get to the department before the deadline. I always send my application packs registered mail, so I get a receipt that they actually got it.

Take one last look to see if everything is neat and spelled right and, most importantly, completed.

Make yourself 6 copies of the entire package.

Okay, send it in. The first step is done; you still have more work to do. It really gets fun now!

Chapter Fifteen: Now the Fun Starts

Remember when I said that grants are competitive? Well, they really are! It has been estimated by professional grant writers that for each grant awarded there are 10 grant applications. In some cases, even more than that!

This chapter will tell you how to get to the top of that list.

Get on the department website and find the name and phone number of the grant manager or grant administrator or project manager. Every department has someone who manages the grant section. They may use different titles, but there is always someone.

Call that person and tell them that you have just sent in a grant application. They will probably ask you about the project. Get enthusiastic and tell them about it. Ask them to take a look at it and give you some help on it. You'll be surprised how helpful these people are. They really want you to get that grant. If you think about it, without people to grant money to they wouldn't have a job!

The grant manager may very well have some changes they would like to see in your grant. Make them! These people know grants inside and out, take their advice.

The next thing you need to do is get the name and address of each of your state legislators. You probably have 1 or 2 state senators and 1-2 state representatives. Write them a letter and tell them that you have applied for a grant; tell them what the grant will do for the voters in their district; and ask them for their support in getting the grant.

Again, you'll be amazed at the response to this. Politicians love to look like they are helping their voters. This one isn't all that hard for them to do. Just a phone call or note to the department is all it takes. The affect on the department is astounding also! After all, this is where they get their money! They will listen to a legislator.

Now, get the name and address of the chairman of your county commission or governing board and write them a letter almost identical to the legislator letter you wrote earlier. These people can make phone calls in support of your grant. Their motivation is that the more money that is granted to a county, the more the economy prospers. The more the economy prospers, the greater the chance they will be re-elected. See how it works?

Let your local paper know about your grant application. Give them a copy of your project summary. Most local papers are starved for local news. You may be surprised at the article you get from just this one thing.

You see, you need to make yourself stand out without being obnoxious. The process, after you apply, is probably more important than the application itself. If you have a good project, a good application and good political follow-up, your chances are greatly improved for a grant award.

Chapter Sixteen: The Outcome

Well, you've applied and you've followed up with the political side of things. Now you wait.

You may very well get a letter asking you to change something about your grant. Take the advice and change it accordingly. Remember, they want to grant you the money!

You may very well get a letter saying that your grant has been denied for the following reasons. Take those reasons to heart. Look at your process and see where you went wrong. Make the applicable changes and re-apply!

AND...you may very well get a letter that your grant application has been approved! Make sure that everyone you contacted about your grant gets a copy of the award letter...don't forget the newspaper! Thank them! You will probably need them again for your next grant.

Once you have been awarded a grant, make sure you do everything that is required by the grant. Turn in the forms, follow up with department frequently, do a great job out there in the field. Make yourself someone who will be much more apt to get another grant next time.

Once you get the process right, you can just plug in projects and repeat it. There is literally no limit to your grant funded projects. Just remember, if you do a good service for the public and can prove that you do, you will always find money somewhere in the grant system.

Chapter Seventeen: Special Federal Grants

As I said earlier, there are a few Federal Grants that are available to individuals. They are extremely narrow in their focus and are VERY, VERY competitive. They are worth mentioning here because they are attainable, but it can take years to get them.

If you are an inventor and have an invention that fits the needs of the U.S. Government, there may be some funding for you.

Before you do anything, make sure that you have a legal patent or have a patent pending on the invention. The patent area is a subject for an entire book in itself. Just be aware of the many "rip-offs" in this area and really do your research on any company that offers to help you get a patent.

Another area of interest to the Federal Government is the ability to take research and development products and make them available to the public at large. Again, this is highly competitive, but highly profitable. I personally know a fellow who was able to take a NASA technology and transfer it to the consumer market. The process took almost 5 years, but he was able to get some funding along the way to support his company until it could make a profit.

This is known as technology transfer. Most major universities have a program or a department that deals with this area.

Go to: http://www.grants.gov/FindGrantOpportunities
To get more details on grants that are available for these two areas.

On that page, there is a search function. For some odd reason, the only way to get a complete listing of all grants available is to change the "Dates of Search" window to 8 weeks. Why, I don't know, but it works!

The last time I searched that site there were 357 possible grants available. It makes for some very technical reading, but if you are in the fields in which they are interested, it should be a breeze for you. It gave me a headache!

If you are interested in technology transfer, the premier institution in the nation is the Robert C. Byrd National Technology Transfer Center, located in Wheeling, West Virginia. They get a huge amount of Federal funds to help you get an invention to market. I know a few people who are on staff there. They are all very willing to help and are very knowledgeable. I recommend the center highly.
The website is: http://www.nttc.edu/

Information on both research/development and technology transfer is also available at The Small Business Administration website, http://www.sba.gov/sbir/

There are a lot of opportunities here, if you are in the technical area. Check it out; it could get you some money! A great way to get started is to call your U.S. Senator's office and ask for help…they are very interested in helping you!

Chapter Eighteen: Worldwide Grants

The United States is not, by far, the only country giving grants. There are some major programs throughout the world that will be very helpful to your cause if you are a resident of the sponsoring country.

I have not, personally, received a grant from any of the organizations listed below. However, I am in contact with people that have and they assure me that the process is nearly identical to the one I've described in this book.

European Union

http://www.eugrants.org/frametemplate.html

Australia

http://www.grantslink.gov.au/

Worldwide

http://www.worldbank.org/rmc/jsdf/index.htm

Worldwide

http://web.worldbank.org/WBSITE/EXTERNAL/OPPORTUNITIES/GRANTS/DEVM ARKETPLACE/0,,menuPK:180652~pagePK:180657~piPK:180651~theSitePK:205098,00. html

Please feel free to contact me if you have had any dealings with these organizations, either negatively or positively.

Chapter Nineteen: Wrapping It All Up

At the very beginning of this book I promised you the truth. Well, you have it!

Grants are not the easiest things to receive. The majority of people who apply don't know how to apply in the first place and are turned down.

You now have the tools and a plan to be awarded a grant if your project is worthy. I have tried to help you zero in on a worthy project; I hope I have succeeded. I know I have given you the correct advice that will work for a good project.

I admire you for going through this process. I'm also a bit envious, because I know what it feels like to be passionate about an idea and be wrapped up in it.

I urge you to try to achieve your dream project. If you can't get a grant, come back and I can show you how to get a loan that's virtually guaranteed.

I hope you have enjoyed this book; it was a pleasure writing it for you. I know that it will help you on your journey to success.

Wishing you success in everything!
Dennis Lively

Chapter Twenty: References

State Economic Development Pages

Alabama http://www.edpa.org/

Alaska http://www.dced.state.ak.us/cbd/home.htm

Arizona http://www.azcommerce.com/default.html

Arkansas http://www.aedc.state.ar.us/home.cfm

California http://commerce.ca.gov/state/ttca/

Colorado http://www.state.co.us/oed/guide/

Connecticut http://www.state.ct.us/ecd/

Delaware http://www.state.de.us/dedo/

Florida http://www.eflorida.com/

Georgia http://www.georgia.org/economic/index.asp

Hawaii http://www.state.hi.us/dbedt/

Idaho http://www.idoc.state.id.us/

Illinois http://www.commerce.state.il.us/

Indiana http://www.in.gov/doc/

Iowa http://www.state.ia.us/ided/

Kansas http://kdoch.state.ks.us/ProgramApp/index_mm.jsp

Kentucky http://www.edc.state.ky.us/

Louisiana http://www.lded.state.la.us/

Maine http://www.econdevmaine.com/

Maryland http://www.choosemaryland.org/

Massachusetts http://www.massconnect.state.ma.us/

Michigan http://medc.michigan.org/index

Minnesota http://www.dted.state.mn.us/01x00f.asp

Mississippi http://www.decd.state.ms.us/

Missouri http://www.ded.state.mo.us/business/business.shtml

Montana http://www.commerce.state.mt.us/l

Nebraska http://assist.neded.org/

Nevada http://www.expand2nevada.com/newsite/index.html

New Hampshire http://www.nheconomy.com/

New Jersey http://www.state.nj.us/commerce/

New Mexico http://www.edd.state.nm.us/

New York http://www.empire.state.ny.us/

North Carolina http://www.commerce.state.nc.us/

North Dakota http://www.growingnd.com/

Ohio http://www.odod.state.oh.us/

Oklahoma http://www.odoc.state.ok.us/index.html

Oregon http://www.oregon.gov/prod/index.cfm%3FCurrPID=502

Pennsylvania   http://www.inventpa.com/default.asp%3Fpath=Business%2520in
%2520PA

Rhode Island http://www.riedc.com/startframe.html

South Carolina http://www.callsouthcarolina.com/callsc.cfm?page=&document=home

South Dakota http://www.sdgreatprofits.com/

Tennessee http://www.state.tn.us/ecd/

Texas http://www.tded.state.tx.us/

Utah http://dced.utah.gov/

Vermont http://thinkvermont.com/

Virginia http://www.yesvirginia.org/

Washington http://www.cted.wa.gov/DesktopDefault.aspx

West Virginia http://www.wvdo.org/business/index.html

Wisconsin http://www.commerce.state.wi.us/

Wyoming http://www.wyomingeda.org/

Official State Pages

Alabama   http://www.alabama.gov/

Alaska   http://www.state.ak.us/

Arizona   http://www.az.gov/webapp/portal/

Arkansas   http://www.accessarkansas.org/

California   http://www.ca.gov/

Colorado   http://www.colorado.gov/

Connecticut http://www.ct.gov/

Delaware   http://www.delaware.gov/

Florida   http://www.myflorida.com/

Georgia   http://www.georgia.gov/

Hawaii   http://www.ehawaiigov.org/

Idaho   http://www.accessidaho.org/

Illinois   http://www.illinois.gov/

Indiana   http://www.in.gov/

Iowa   http://www.state.ia.us/

Kansas   http://www.accesskansas.org/

Kentucky   http://www.kentucky.gov/

Louisiana   http://www.state.la.us/

Maine   http://www.maine.gov/

Maryland   http://www.maryland.gov/

Massachusetts   http://www.mass.gov/

Michigan   http://www.michigan.gov/

Minnesota   http://www.state.mn.us/

Mississippi   http://www.ms.gov/

Missouri   http://www.state.mo.us/

Montana   http://www.discoveringmontana.com/

Nebraska   http://www.nol.org/

Nevada   http://www.nv.gov/

New Hampshire http://www.state.nh.us/

New Jersey   http://www.state.nj.us/

New Mexico http://www.state.nm.us/

New York   http://www.state.ny.us/

North Carolina http://www.ncgov.com/

North Dakota   http://www.discovernd.com/

Ohio   http://www.state.oh.us/

Oklahoma   http://www.youroklahoma.com/

Oregon   http://www.oregon.gov/

Pennsylvaniahttp://www.state.pa.us/

Rhode Island http://www.ri.gov/

South Carolina http://www.myscgov.com/

South Dakota http://www.state.sd.us/

Tennessee http://www.tennesseeanytime.org/

Texas http://www.texasonline.com/

Utah http://www.utah.gov/

Vermont http://www.vermont.gov/

Virginia http://www.myvirginia.org/

Washington http://access.wa.gov/

West Virginia http://www.state.wv.us/

Wisconsin http://www.wisconsin.gov/

Wyoming http://www.state.wy.us/

State Grants Pages

Alabama   http://www.arts.state.al.us/

           http://www.preserveala.org/

Alaska   http://www.educ.state.ak.us/aksca/

               http://www.eed.state.ak.us/lam/

Arizona   http://www.arizonaarts.org/

           http://www.dlapr.lib.az.us/

Arkansas   http://www.arkansasarts.com/

           http://www.arkansasheritage.com/

California   http://www.caam.ca.gov/

              http://www.cac.ca.gov/

Colorado   http://www.coloarts.state.co.us/

http://www.coloradohistory.org/

Connecticut http://www.ctarts.org/
http://www.ctfreedomtrail.com/

Delaware http://www.artsdel.org/
http://www.state.de.us/sos/archives.htm

Hawaii http://www.state.hi.us/sfca/
http://www.hcc.hawaii.edu/hspls/

Idaho http://www2.state.id.us/arts/
http://www.idahohistory.net/

Illinois http://www.finditillinois.org/
http://www.state.il.us/agency/iac/

Indiana http://www.in.gov/arts/
http://www.statelib.lib.in.us/

Iowa http://www.culturalaffairs.org/
http://www.iowaartscouncil.org/

Kansas http://www.kshs.org/
http://skyways.lib.ks.us/kansas/KSL/

| Kentucky | http://eah.ky.gov/ |
| | http://www.kyarts.org/ |

Kentucky http://eah.ky.gov/
          http://www.kyarts.org/

Louisiana http://www.crt.state.la.us/
           http://lafilm.org/

Maine http://www.mainearts.com/
       http://www.state.me.us/mhpc/

Maryland http://www.mpt.org/
          http://www.msac.org/

Massachusetts http://www.state.ma.us/lib/

Michigan http://www.michigan.gov/hal
          http://www.michigan.gov/hal/0,1607,7-160-17445_19272---,00.html

Minnesota http://www.mnhs.org/
           http://www.arts.state.mn.us/

Mississippi http://www.mdah.state.ms.us/
             http://www.arts.state.ms.us/

Missouri http://www.missouriartscouncil.org/
          http://www.sos.mo.gov/library/

Montana   http://art.state.mt.us/

                 http://www.his.state.mt.us/

Nebraska   http://www.nebraskaartscouncil.org/

                 http://www.nlc.state.ne.us/

Nevada   http://dmla.clan.lib.nv.us/

                 http://dmla.clan.lib.nv.us/docs/arts/

New Hampshire http://webster.state.nh.us/nhculture/

                 http://www.state.nh.us/nharts/

New Jersey   http://www.njstatelib.org/

New Mexico http://www.nmoca.org/

                 http://www.stlib.state.nm.us/

New York   http://www.nysca.org/

                 http://www.archives.nysed.gov/

North Carolina http://www.ncdcr.gov/

                 http://www.ncarts.org/

North Dakota   http://www.state.nd.us/arts/

                 http://www.state.nd.us/hist/

Ohio   http://www.oac.state.oh.us/

http://winslo.state.oh.us/

Oklahoma   http://www.odl.state.ok.us/
http://www.oklaosf.state.ok.us/~arts/

Oregon   http://www.oregonartscommission.org/
http://www.osl.state.or.us/home/

Pennsylvaniahttp://www.phmc.state.pa.us/
http://www.artsnet.org/pca/

Rhode Island http://www.state.ri.us/archives/

http://www.risca.state.ri.us/

South Carolina http://www.state.sc.us/scdah/

http://www.state.sc.us/arts/

South Dakota   http://www.state.sd.us/deca/

http://www.sdarts.org/

Tennessee   http://www.arts.state.tn.us/

http://www.state.tn.us/film/

Texas   http://www.arts.state.tx.us/

http://www.thc.state.tx.us/

Virgin Islands   http://www.library.gov.vi/

Utah   http://arts.utah.gov/

http://www.archives.utah.gov/

Vermont   http://www.vermontartscouncil.org/

http://www.vermonthistory.org/

Virginia   http://www.arts.state.va.us/

http://www.dhr.state.va.us/

Washington   http://www.statelib.wa.gov/

http://www.arts.wa.gov/

West Virginia   http://www.wvosea.org/

http://www.wvculture.org/

http://www.wvculture.org/arts/index.html

Wisconsin   http://www.wisconsinhistory.org/

http://arts.state.wi.us/static/

Wyoming   http://wyoarts.state.wy.us/

http://spacr.state.wy.us/

Other Useful Resources

http://www.sba.gov

http://www.cyberatlas.com

http://www.microcreditsummit.org/forms/database.htm

http://www.usembassy.state.gov

http://www.sba.gov/financing/microparticipants.html

Great Loan Calculator

http://www.finaid.org/calculators/loanpayments.phtml

I hope you feel like you

got a lot out of this book...

I sure put a LOT into it!

If you did,

PLEASE tell your friends about it!

You can see more of my books at

www.DennisLively.com

You can also write to me directly there

by using the "Contact Dennis" link.

I'd genuinely LOVE to hear from you!

Thanks for the trust you put in me

when you bought this book.

I promise you I'll ALWAYS strive

to continue earning it!

Dennis

www.ingramcontent.com/pod-product-compliance
Lightning Source LLC
Chambersburg PA
CBHW071637170526
45166CB00003B/1353